CW01082254

This one goes out to the ones I love.

The courageous storytellers who dare to connect minds and open hearts. The ones who weave together tremendous sentences, invite us into their spheres, open up galaxies and remind us of our humanity.

This book is dedicated to us.

Published by
Electron Unlimited LLC
8415 5th Ave NE #305
Seattle, WA 98115

©2023 Jeff Leisawitz / Electron Unlimited LLC
Illustrations ©Megan Hills • Layout and design by Jeff
Leisawitz
ISBN 979-8-9887640-0-7

For ordering information or special discounts
for bulk purchases, educational use or fund-
raising, please contact Jeff Leisawitz at
Jeff@JeffLeisawitz.com

CONTENTS

The Upside to Being a Weird Friendless
Kid

Icebergs, Cavemen and Blue Aliens

Aretha's Secret Ingredient

The Magic of Transformation

The Most Famous Teenage Dropout

The Craptacular Babbler Chills Out

Amplify the Magic

The Alchemy of Golden Repair

Become the Gift

Where the Rubber Meets the Road

Tramps Like Us

The Upside to Being a Weird Friendless Kid

I was a weird friendless kid.

Flash back to second grade. Art class. The teacher gives us some brand new crayons. These are very fancy, oil based, really bright crayons. So coooool.

She tells the kids, "Go ahead. Draw whatever you want. Be creative."

So, my muggle-in-training classmates make a mess trying to sketch out a bunch of rainbows and flowers and suns with smiley faces. Stuff like that.

I thought it would be smart to draw upside down UFOs with these Frankenstein guys driving them. Of course! Beaming with pride and joy, I deliver my masterpiece to the teacher. So cool!

She did not think it was so cool. In fact, she sent me to the guidance counselor for a psych eval.

Fast forward a few years. Now it's fourth grade.

I'm starting to get bullied. I have a birth defect—a lazy eye. My eyelid doesn't open the whole way and I blink too much.

These kids are really mean and nasty. They call me all kinds of names and make me feel shitty.

But there was some good news. I was into *The Six Million Dollar Man* at the time. That was a seventies TV show about a guy who crashed a rocket in a very big way. But the feds had a plan.

And so did I.

I told those kids I had a bionic eye. And if they didn't get out of there, I was gonna get bionic on their ass.

Fast forward a few more years. Junior high.

As usual, I'm loitering in the hallway, when this new girl shows up. She's from Chicago. She is very cool. As in, very, very cool. Obviously not from around here.

Half her head is shaved, the other half is dyed bright red. She's decked out like she just stepped out of an eighties music video. And no joke, her name is Amber Savage.

I was in love. (But she didn't know I existed.)

So, I went home that night and I did the only thing that made any sense to my hormone addled brain cell. I penned a love note to her and jammed it in my pocket.

When I went to school the next day I was way too scared to give it to her. So I kept it in my pocket for days, weeks. Finally, one day I saw her in the lunch line all by herself.

I scurried over and gave her the note. Then I got the hell out of there.

I hid in the corner at the empty table where I'd normally have lunch. From afar, I watched her sit down with all of her popular girl friends.

She took out the note, read it, and started giggling. She passed it around. Her friends laughed and pointing at me.

It was a total heartbreaker. Devastating.

But I realized something in that moment. Despite the fact that that fourteen year old hellcat had just stomped my heart, I loved *writing* that love letter.

So I kept writing. I've written stories and songs, screenplays, poems, blog posts, books, haikus, journal entries, whatever. If words are involved, I'm in.

Over the decades, I've banged my head against the wall in pursuit of the truth…

Why is storytelling such a big deal? Why is it so important? How does it connect us?

I've banged my head against the wall. There has been blood. By the end of this book, I hope to help you bang your head against the wall a little less.

In these pages, I'm gonna riff about the magical impact of storytelling—the magic of transformation.

I'm gonna monologue about the *why* that drives our stories. Because when we know the *why* we can activate the magic.

And finally, I'm gonna talk some big talk about the deep truth of storytelling.

Because at its core, storytelling is a way for us to be seen, expressed, healed and connected.

Why does this matter? Because in that moment when Amber Savage and her savage pals were laughing at me, I felt so alone.

But I was not alone. Not really.

Because as writers, we're in this together. We're on a mission to open minds and connect hearts with our words and stories.

And why does this matter? Because now more than ever, the world needs to come together. And whether we know it or not, we are magical creatures.

There's magic in your pen, in your paper, in your pixels. In your melodies and images.

This is a big deal. I know it because I coach it. I write it. I dream it. I am it. And for the next however many pages, I'm gonna write it. And if all goes well, you're gonna get it.

Dig it?

Icebergs, Cavemen and Blue Aliens

So, what does it really mean to tell a story? To be an author?

Author = Authority

That's the authority to create worlds.

Think about that for a minute. The authority to create worlds— whether that's a book, movie, song or video.

And when we author well, our audiences forget they're even listening to our songs, or reading our stories, or watching our content.

Remember when Kate and Leo were holding on for dear life to the railings of the Titanic as it's about to plunge into the endless black frozen ocean?

Yeah, you kind of forgot that you were sitting there in the theater or laying around on your couch in your underwear. Even now when I watch that movie and I see those musicians playing as the ship goes down, I get kinda weepy.

But here's the thing. I was not on the Titanic. And you were not on the Titanic. But we experienced a story on the Titanic from a safe place.

That's one of the magical aspects of storytelling. We can experience something dangerous from a safe place. Through a story, through a song, through a movie.

We can get lost in the jungle. We can explore outer space. We can tap into the enlightened heart of a stranger or the twisted mind of a killer.

Let's flash back to the cavemen.

It's a dark and stormy night. There's a fire blazing in the cave. Experienced hunters are trying to tell a story to the young men who've never been on a hunt before.

They're jumping around. Grunting. They're painting the cave walls. They're trying to explain that there is a wild beast out there somewhere. And if you don't follow the plan, it'll kill you and eat your guts for lunch.

So, here's the scoop… We're gonna surround this thing. When the chief says go, we're all gonna bust out our spears. We're all gonna attack this unholy beast at the same time. If we do this right, we'll go home as heroes with full bellies.

The young, inexperienced hunters in that cave could experience the hunt without the danger. From a safe place. This is a magical aspect of storytelling.

The good news is that there are not a whole lot of wild beasts running around the countryside these days. But there are a whole lot of things in life that we might want to experience as stories, as songs, as movies—before we experience them IRL.

We can even learn from a mediocre romantic comedy. In your basic romantic comedy the young woman needs to choose between the jerky rich guy and the nerd who loves her.

Or let's take a trip to a faraway planet. To Pandora, where those blue aliens might teach us a thing or two about honoring our planet and its environment.

So, whether we're on the Titanic or back with the cavemen or in a romantic comedy or on Pandora, I would suggest that it takes a whole lot of imagination to author fiction. To author anything.

In our imaginations we can fly. We can breathe underwater. We can time travel. This is what writers do. And I would say that imagination is just a half step away from magic.

I've always believed in magic. When I was a little kid, I did magic shows at other kids' birthday parties.

I used to teach magic tricks to my gluten-free ex-girlfriend's eight year old boy. That kid called me The Wizard.

You may call me a weirdo, but I believe in magic. I believe in astrology and psychic phenomenon and quantum realities. Stuff like that.

I'm not talking about the kind of magic like pulling a rabbit out of a hat or levitating above a picnic table. I'm talking about the kind of magic where we connect minds and open hearts with our words and our stories.

When we write with power and passion and intention, our stories become infused with our magic. That's the magic of transformation—another magical aspect of storytelling.

Because, at its core, storytelling is a way for us to be seen, expressed, healed and connected. And when we are seen, expressed, healed and connected through our stories, we transform. And so do our readers and our audiences.

I just might be a dreamer, but I doubt I'm the only one.

Are you with me?

Aretha's Secret Ingredient

Why do we write? And why do we write the stories that we do?

If you don't know the answer to this question, you'll never be able to fully activate your magic to connect minds and open hearts.

Knowing your *why* is such a big deal because it focuses your intention. And intention drives action.

But here's the thing. At the end of the day there are only two factors that really influence human behavior. That's *fear* and *love*. You can stack all kinds of other stuff on top of those things, but when you boil it all down, everything is driven by fear or love, or some combination.

You may fear oppression and love freedom. You may fear helplessness and love helpfulness.

That's why it's so important to know what really drives you. Knowing your *why* is a freaking huge deal. They actually carved it in stone at the Temple at Delphi.

Know Thyself

When you know yourself deeply you can activate your magic to connect minds and open hearts with your words and stories.

Let's flashback again.

When I was a little kid I needed surgery on my malfunctioning eyelid. My parents thought it would be a good idea to talk to a couple of different doctors and interview them to see which one might be best for this delicate operation.

They went to check out the first guy. He was well known and respected in the community. They sat in his office and talked to him about the procedure and asked him a bunch of questions.

They noticed that the doc was wearing a thousand dollar suit. He had pictures all over his office of his fancy cars, his yacht, his swanky vacations.

And this guy had some cutting edge technology on his wrist. A digital watch.

Soon after, my folks went to talk to the next eye surgeon. This woman was also at the top of her game. They asked her all kinds of questions. She was totally legit.

By the end of their time together, they were getting friendly. So, my dad asked her, "Why did you decide to become an eye surgeon?"

This woman said that when she was a little kid, she was home alone with her twin sister. Somehow the sister got into the cleaning products.

Her sister managed to splash some bleach in her eye. Her sister was freaking out, screaming, crying. She didn't know how to help. She was a clueless kid.

By the time their mom got home, her sister's vision was starting to deteriorate. The family watched helplessly for the next few weeks

as her twin went completely
blind in one eye.

So, when she grew up, this
woman decided that she wanted
to become an eye doctor. To help
other people who were going
through similar traumas.

Which one of these eye surgeons
would you choose to operate on
your child?

Okay, let's port this over to
another one of my favorite
topics—pop music.

In your typical pop song the
singer generally has at least half
a clue (or they auto-tune the
vocals). There's a decent melody.
It might even be an earworm. But
most pop songs disappear into
the ethers within a few months
and you never hear them again.

Flash back. This time to the early seventies. We're in New York City and a young woman is walking to a recording studio.

This woman had her first child at age twelve.

This woman was arrested at a civil rights demonstration for disturbing the peace. When she got out, she said something like, "Black people will be free. Sometimes you gotta disturb the peace when you can't get no peace."

Decades later, *Rolling Stone* magazine declared the song that she was about to sing to be the fifth best song ever recorded.

So, when the Queen of Soul stepped up to that microphone that day, she definitely knew her *why*.

She knew her fear and she knew her love. Her oppression and her freedom. The sexism and racism that had been haunting her whole life.

And then she belted it all into that microphone—
R E S P E C T!

When Aretha Franklin sang, the world listened.

When you listen to that song now, you'll hear the passion and fire, the purpose, the intention. The *why*. In fifty more years, when people listen to that song, they're still gonna hear it loud and clear.

We need to write like Aretha sings.

Whether it's songs, movies, stories, books, blog posts, content or marketing copy.

We need to write like Aretha sings.

Or makes movies like James Cameron.

His love and fascination of the ocean fueled his passion for making the epic tale of the Titanic. His fear of killer robots, AI and technology pointed him toward The Terminator movies. And the Avatar franchise speaks to his love of nature, this planet and his concerns that we are destroying our only world.

These kinds of drivers are huge. They make these projects more than jobs. More than paychecks. More than the glitz and glamour and spectacle.

When you see a big Hollywood movie with all kinds of splashy special effects but no real heart or soul, you can feel it. It might look cool, but does it make you feel anything? The *why*, when fully activated by a writer or creator, amplifies the emotional energy exponentially.

Taylor Swift knows this. Besides being incredibly gifted with her music, her business savvy and her performances, Ms. Swift writes songs that matter to her. Really matter to her.

She articulates the painful truths of her love life. She reveals the fears, insecurities, dramas and heart break of being a young woman in the spotlight. She knows the emotional devastation of being criticized mercilessly in public. And going home alone.

She writes her songs because her pain drives her. To be seen. Expressed. Healed. Connected.

This is her *why*. And a whole lot of people can relate.

As it turns out, people can relate to many, many different things that affect us all in one way or another. There are many *why's* that drive us.

Why does Stephen King write?

This guy has become one of the most successful authors of all time. His books have sold millions and millions of copies around the globe. They've made movies and tv shows out of his stories. So why does Stephen King write?

The King of Horror has said
again and again in interviews
throughout the decades that he
writes horror because, as a child,
he was so scared. Scared of the
dark. Scared of the world. Scared
of the monsters and paranormal
and darkness within each of us.

But at the same time, he was
attracted to these things.

Why might that be? Why would
anyone be attracted to what
scares them? What hurts them?
What amplifies the darkness
inside of them?

Humans have a peculiar
psychological quirk. Ok, fine.
We have many. But this is the
one that sort of leads the moth to
the flame. Not in a quest towards
death, but in a quest to heal.

By untangling our pain and our fear in our stories and creativity, we heal ourselves. And our audience.

This is the big transformation that's possible in our stories, songs, movies, art. And life.

But I'm getting ahead of myself. More on this in the next chapter.

The Magic of Transformation

You may have heard of a gentleman named Joseph Campbell. Joseph Campbell is famous for a number of things. Probably his biggest deal is an idea called 'The Hero's Journey.' Or what I sometimes like to call 'The Heroine's Journey.'

The hero or heroine's journey is when a Greek god or goddess type hears the call to adventure and heads out on a difficult, dangerous and daunting task to slay some kind of dragon.

They transform internally and externally and come back changed. They come back a hero.

That's great if you're a Greek god or goddess type. But this is kind of tricky for us mere mortals. We tend to not want to go on difficult, dangerous or daunting adventures.

Why would we even do this?

Because it's the only way to truly and deeply change. To transform. To activate the magic and infuse it in into our creativity to connect minds and to open hearts.

*

My mom is a straight up great lady. And unlike me, she's seriously straight down the middle. Very 'normal.' She never really got me as a storyteller, a musician, a creative.

However, when my mom was in college, her roommate was a woman who would eventually become a full-time visual artist. These two have been in touch for decades. So, a couple years ago, my mom calls her up.

"Hey, Syma. How's it going?"

"Well, last year was fantastic. I had all these amazing ideas. I made a ton of money. But this year, not so much. I'm scraping the curb. I just can't find my flow."

My mom asks her, "Why would you choose a life like this?"

"Because it hurts me when I don't create."

Wow.

A few weeks later I'm talking to my mom and she tells me about this conversation. She asks me, "Does it hurt you when you don't create?"

"No, not even close, not at all. It kills me slowly. It destroys my heart. It sucks the blood from my soul."

I must create. And you must create too, if you feel this call to adventure. Because this is the way we transform our characters. Our stories. Ourselves.

And this will help our readers and listeners and viewers transform themselves. To connect minds, open hearts.

So this begs the question…

What does a great story actually do?

The Most Famous Teenage Drop Out

A great story elevates you into worlds of joy. It smears you with fear. It swirls your brains with big ideas.

A great story smashes your heart through your tears.

A great story threads together tremendous sentences to launch you into a new space, where you can experience a new race. Or a new gender.

Where we can learn about ourselves. And the world. And each other… together.

*

So how do we do that? How do we tell a truly great story?

It always starts with our personal perspective.

Dig this. Out of the billions and billions of humans who have walked the earth, you are literally the only one who has ever experienced your exact life.

And at the same time, every human who has ever lived shares common themes with you. Themes of survival, themes of love and community, loss of innocence, mortality. And many other challenges.

This is one of the top secrets to authoring a story that's going to land in the center of your audience's heart.

You must intersect your personal perspective with universal themes of human experience.

It's a big idea. I know. Chew slowly.

Flash back again.

This time I'm in college. It's a beautiful Tuesday afternoon. My girlfriend at the time and I decide to cut class. Of course.

We grab some ice cream. She gets a ton of rainbow sprinkles on hers. We head on down to the park. We're kind of standing on this little bridge watching these four ducks swim in a row right in front of us. It's a beautiful day. Perfect.

She turns to me and says, "It's over."

What the f? So harsh.

Question. Has anyone out there in book-land ever experienced this exact same story? You cut class on a Tuesday afternoon in the fall in college with your boyfriend or girlfriend. Find your way to some ice cream with a ton of sprinkles. Stand on a bridge and watch four ducks. And then out of nowhere, the other person just pulls the plug.

Have you ever experienced that exact same story? I doubt it. It sort of can't happen because there are too many specific details.

But let me ask you another question.

Have you ever been dumped?

Yeah. Oops. Sucks.

That's the universal human theme—rejection.

When we connect and intersect these two concepts—the personal perspective and the universal theme—that's the sweet spot. Another magical aspect of storytelling.

It reminds me of my favorite book, *The Catcher in the Rye,* by J. D. Salinger. This is a book about a rich kid in the fifties in New York City who's getting kicked out of prep school.

I wasn't even close to a rich kid who got kicked out of prep school in New York City in the fifties. In fact, I wasn't even hanging around on earth yet. But that's where the author came from. That was his world. That's where he lived.

As a reader, I can't personally relate to the 'rich kid in New York' stuff. But the universal themes in this book resonate with me bigtime. Themes of navigating a complex world. Questioning authority. And spotting the phonies.

J. D. Salinger expertly connected his experience with these universal challenges. The result is a book that has been read by millions and millions of people across decades and languages. He effectively opened minds and connected hearts through his words and stories.

This is the magical impact of storytelling.

So why is it so freaking hard to write a great story like this?

The Craptacular Babbler Chills Out

As a life coach for storytellers of every flavor, I've encountered all kinds of challenges in my clients. But there's one thing that typically comes to the top of the list every single time.

A few years ago, I had a client who was working on a memoir. This was a very difficult story—about the death of her stillborn child.

She would say to me, "Jeff, I just can't do this. I hear this voice in my head that says this is too hard. And who wants to read my story anyway?"

We did all kinds of guided meditations, practices, exercises. Then she wrote her book. She claims that writing it helped her heal from this very difficult trauma. (And BTW, she now has a healthy young daughter and her memoir topped two Amazon best seller lists!)

So, what was that voice that she heard in her head that was keeping her down?

It's called the *Inner Critic*. I'm sure you're familiar with this guy.

*

So, what is the inner critic? And why is it lodged in our heads?

The inner critic is actually such a big deal that I wrote an entire chapter about it in my book, *Not F*ing Around— The No Bullsh*t Guide for Getting your Creative Dreams Off the Ground.*

The inner critic is one of the 'parts' of our psychology. Even though we may not like it, it's there for a reason—to keep us safe. The problem is that it generally speaks too loudly and at inappropriate times.

Imagine that we're hanging out at the Grand Canyon. It's midnight. There's a storm raging. Thunder and lightning all over the place. You and I have a bottle of whiskey. Of course. We're passing it around.
Then I get a great idea! I'll do some cartwheels right at the edge of the Grand Canyon.

My inner critic speaks up and says, "Hey, maybe that's not such a great idea."

This would be a good time to listen to my inner critic.

However, let's say you're about to put out a social media post and you decide that it would be kind of cool to conjure up a new word that has never before been uttered in the English language.

Your inner critic starts shouting. "No, no, no! Don't do it. Someone out there on the internet might not like it." This is a time to quiet your inner critic. To ignore its ramblings.

So how do we get a handle on our inner critic?

Well, the first step is really pretty simple. We need to name it. Because when we name something, we have a sense of control over it. A sense of ownership.

As you may know if you read my other book, I like to call my inner critic 'The Ic.' That's short for Inner Critic.

But sometimes I call it "The Little Snotball." I also tend to go with a few other names like "Mr. Corned Beef" or "The Craptacular Babbler" or simply, "Yap Yap the Ass Hat."

So let's take a minute to write down some nicknames for your inner critic. Be creative, go wild. Use profanity if you must.

…

Okay, so now you have a few names for your inner critic. Fantastic. Here's where it gets a little weird and a little bit counterintuitive.

Generally when we don't like a part of ourselves, we try to push it away or smash it underneath so it doesn't affect us. Then we can't see it and we don't have to acknowledge it. Good plan, right?

Nope. As a life coach (and a human who has tried it many times), I can guarantee you with 100% certainty that this is not going to work in the long run.

Instead, we need to invite this psychological part back to the party. To integrate it more fully into our consciousness and personality. Because every psychological part of us, at its core, is trying to help and contribute to our highest good.

So how do we do this? Simple. We exclaim our love for the part. As in…

"I love you, Mr. Corned Beef!"

or

"I love you, Craptacular Babbler!"

So, here's your big chance to practice. Please, please actually do this. No one is listening.

You already have your nickname for your inner critic. So just say it out loud.

"I love you, _____."

It feels weirdly good, right? Maybe kind of uncomfortable, but still kinda warm and fuzzy underneath.

Try it again. This time louder. With feeling.

Notice how your inner critic is changing inside of yourself. Perhaps it's softening up. Letting down that nasty edge a bit.

You can call me a hippie. But here's the truth…

You can change any enemy into an ally with love.

This works in all kinds of ways out there in the world. But it works best within ourselves.

Amplify the Magic

Now that we're starting to get a handle on our inner critic, I'd like to circle back to the *why*.

That's "Know Thyself" at the Temple of Delphi. And Aretha singing R-E-S-P-E-C-T. Or that kickass eye surgeon.

As a coach, the first time I ask someone *why* they're telling their story, whether it's a song or a screenplay or a book or anything, I don't get the full answer or the deep truth. It just doesn't happen.

So, I've come up with a little exercise…

1.　　State a fact about your creative life.
2.　　Ask yourself *why* this is true.

3.   Answer the question the best you can.

This is where people typically stop. We wanna take it further. Deeper.

4.   Ask *why* of your answer.
5.   Answer this question with as much vulnerability and honesty as possible.
6.   Lather, rinse, repeat.

I call this process **The Five Why's**.

You certainly don't need to ask yourself *why* all five times. But then again, you may need to ask seven or ten times to finally get to the deep truth of who you are and what's really driving your story.

So let's run through this exercise with myself as an example.

First, I'll start with my statement about my creative life.

I'm a writer, a musician, a screenwriter, a filmmaker and a photographer.

Why?

Because, like Madonna, I want to express myself.

Why?

Because as a kid who sucked at sports and pretty much everything else, I eventually realized there was a likeminded community of creatives out there. And I wanted to hang out with them.

Why was that such a big deal?

Because like everyone reading this book, and everyone in the world (whether they know it or not), I want to be seen, expressed and healed.

Why is this such a big deal?

Because the desire to be seen, expressed and healed is a fundamental human truth. And when we grant ourselves the time and the opportunity to create with authenticity and vulnerability, we open up a space to transform into better versions of ourselves.

Like my old friend Mahatma Gandhi once said, "Be the change you want to see in the world."

Or, as my old pal Neo once remarked, "Be the glitch you want to see in the matrix."

Be the change. Be the glitch.
Know your *why*. Know your
truth.

As my old buddy Bono once
mentioned, "I just need four
chords and the truth."

And if you're not a musician, you
don't even need the chords.

When you combine your truth
with the universal themes that
drive you, the magic amplifies.

As my old friend Billy Joel once
noticed—sharing a drink called
loneliness is better than drinking
alone.

The Alchemy of Golden Repair

I'd like to tell you about a coin I've termed. Or perhaps a term I've coined.

Emotional Perspective.

What is an emotional perspective? An emotional perspective is simply a subjective experience that is intensified by emotion.

We're psychologically built with beliefs about the world and identities about ourselves. Sometimes these things touch on emotions and amplify our experiences. That's an emotional perspective.

Emotional perspectives are powerful. They drive our lives, our choices. And they will magnify your characters and stories.

Here's an example:

On a crappy day, my emotional perspective may be that the world is out to get me. I'm not smart enough, I'm not creative enough, I'm not driven enough to get to my goals.

But on a good day my emotional perspective might be that I am smart enough. I am driven enough. My creativity has something to contribute to the world.

Both of these can certainly feel true. Both of these are accurate emotional perspectives if I feel them. But here's where it gets interesting.

Humans can experience and feel opposite things at the same time. We can feel capable and incapable in the same moment. We can feel fear and excitement. At one time or another, we've all savored the confounding flavor of bittersweet.

This is called *cognitive dissonance*. Cognitive dissonance is when two opposing ideas that are both true are held within us at the same time, in the same moment.

As my old friend Walt Whitman once said, "I am large. I contain multitudes."

I think that's what he was talking about. I am large, I contain multitudes. And so do you.

Here's the thing. Cognitive dissonance and emotional

perspectives are written all over our psyches. When we infuse these things into our characters, into our songs, and into our words, it creates a massive space for transformation, growth, and change.

I recently wrote a new screenplay. This baby is called *Tales of Summers Past*. It's a retro comedy about my twelve summers in the woods in the seventies and eighties at Camp Log-n-Twig. It was a real place. Look it up.

Here are the main characters in the story—

Tuna is a clueless counselor who just can't get the girl.

Wildflower is a stoner guitar player who's always going for the big dream.

Jen is a pretty teenager who is scared to show her true self to the world.

Her friend Glossy is a punk rock weirdo who doesn't care what anybody else thinks.

And the last character is Teeth, a sweetheart ten-year-old boy who is being relentlessly bullied.

Does this sound like anyone you kind of, sort of, maybe know?

When we infuse our characters with personal stories and emotional perspectives, and cross them with universal themes, and add in the cognitive dissonance which exists in all of us, we pretty much instantly activate the magic to open minds and connect hearts.

This works whether it's stories, screenplays, marketing copy or lyrics.

This takes a ton of vulnerability. I know. It's kind of scary, right?

It reminds me of something that I learned in college. It's a term known as 'golden repair.' In Japanese, the word is *kintsugi*.

I was fortunate enough in college to go on a trip to Japan. I was unfortunate enough to go with the girlfriend with the sprinkles after she dumped me.

But anyway, we went to this museum where they had all these ancient Japanese artifacts. One really stood out for me. It was this beautiful hand painted vase. The thing was cracked all over the place. The cracks were painted and glued together with seams of gold.

This is called kintsugi or 'golden repair' in the Japanese culture. It means that when something is broken and put back together with scars of gold, it becomes more interesting, more precious, more valuable.

This is true for vases. It's also true for humans.

As you may have noticed, life is going to knock you around. So what are you gonna do with that? When you heal yourself and create scars of gold out of your trials and tribulations and traumas, you become more valuable, more precious, more interesting.

And when you fuse that into your characters and stories and songs, you activate the magic to connect minds and open hearts.

Except now the magic is exponential.

Yes, it is scary. It's another magical aspect of storytelling that will super charge your creativity in huge ways. By threading together scars of gold with your tremendous sentences you will activate the magic to connect minds and open hearts.

And you will be seen, expressed, healed and connected.

Becoming the Gift

We've talked a bit about using our stories to be seen, expressed, healed and connected in the previous pages. Now it's time to dig in.

In my experience, we're not particularly well seen.

When you're cruising the freeway or walking down the city street, people do see you. But it's mostly just to avoid crashing into you.

People at work or at the coffee shop or your favorite watering hole might see you. Kind of. They know you a little bit. But generally, they don't really see you or understand you. And often they don't particularly care.

Let's move into your inner circle.
That's your family, your friends,
your lovers, your besties.
Hopefully these people see you
deeply, know you and understand
you. But in my experience, this is
not often the case. They do see
you. But they generally don't see
all of you.

Let's take a look at the word
expressed.

To be expressed simply means
moving from the potential to the
actual.

Think of a dancer who knows all
the moves. But on this particular
Saturday night, she sits in the
corner sipping her drink while
the disco ball spins and the beat
thumps. In this moment, she's
not expressed as a dancer. As
soon as she steps out onto the

dance floor and starts shaking it, she's expressed as a dancer.

The same thing is true for us. You may have a hundred songs on your hard drive. But unless you're actually writing a song, you're not expressed as a songwriter in that moment. Or perhaps you're a poet with a hundred poems on your desk. Again, that's great, but you're not expressed as a poet unless you're actually writing a poem.

Make sense?

Ok, time to talk about this business about being *healed* through our storytelling.

In my experience, and in the experience of literally every creative I've ever spoken to, when we create with truth and depth and vulnerability, there is some kind of healing that happens. It's just part of the process. Part of the magic.

Often this healing can be a catharsis—letting go of something big and dark and heavy and troubling. But it doesn't have to be. The healing can also be a celebration. What's the healing or the celebration in a love song? No more lonely nights.

When we are seen, expressed and healed through our storytelling, we give that gift of our creativity to the world.

But here's where it gets really cool.

When we give our gift to the world, we become the gift.

Because we show others that they can be seen, expressed and healed.

That changes us from a bunch of humans who can thread together tremendous sentences, write poems, craft plots, and weave beautiful melodies—into undercover rock star ninjas who are here to help connect and heal the world.

Some might call me a dreamer, but I kinda doubt that I'm the only one.

Where the Rubber Meets the Road

Okay, so now you've got a plan. You know the deep truth. You understand what your creativity can do, and how powerful it is. But you still have to actually do the thing—write the book, record the song, pen the screenplay.

This is where the rubber meets the road.

As a life coach, I've heard all kinds of challenges from my clients. They say, "Jeff, I don't have enough time. I have these terrible habits. I'm too scared to be vulnerable and really put myself out there."

Okay, okay. I get it. It's true and it does affect us. Let's cut straight to the bone.

Here are the three elements you need to align to do something big, something amazing.

Head.
Heart.
Hands.

The *head* is the intellect. Knowing the *why* that drives you.

Remember the fear and the love and all the things that can be stacked on top? That needs to be part of your consciousness. And firmly lodged in your head.

The second element that must be aligned is the *heart*.

The heart is our emotional experience. If we don't really feel the emotion to step us forward on our creative journey, we'll never be fully activated in our magic. Not only that, we

probably won't have enough
juice to make it to the finish line.
We absolutely must feel the
emotion of our creative vision,
story and/ or mission.

Got the head and heart? Great!

Part three is where tons of people
get stuck—the *hands*.

The hands represent the *action*
we need to conceptualize,
activate and finish our projects.
To actually do the thing.

So how do we do this? We have
to decide to make it happen.

Whatever it is—visualizing an
award-winning ad campaign,
busting out your memoir,
scripting some sweet dialogue—
we must *decide* to do it.

The problem is, when most people decide something, it's generally kind of half assed. Like last night when I decided to have one teeny tiny bite of chocolate.

So how do we make a real decision that's full of passion and purpose and intention?

Let's take the word apart to sherlock up some clues.

The *de-* in 'decide' comes from the Latin. It means 'the opposite.'

And *-cide* means 'to kill.' As in suicide, homicide, genocide.

F.

So, what 'to decide' really means, is to *kill all the other options*. And I can guarantee that when you kill all the other options, you will choose your own adventure and forge your own path.

You will do the thing. You will complete the mission. You will activate your magic to open minds and connect hearts with your words, your stories. Your tremendous sentences.

It reminds me of my old friend Tony Robbins. You know Tony. The big life coach guy. Tony claims that for the past thirty-five years or so, he jumps into an ice bath or takes an ice cold shower. Every. Single. Morning.

Why in the world would anyone do something like that? Because it activates a cascade of hormonal effects, ramps up your dopamine and focus. You feel better. You're energized. The eggheads have studied this. It's science! It's real. I dare you to do it.

I heard Tony talking on a podcast recently. The host asked him about his rather hardcore ice bath habit.

"What kind of a nut job does this? And how in the world have you pulled this off every morning for thirty-five years?"

Tony responds with something very powerful. Something that really resonates with me. Hits me like a sledgehammer.

"I do not negotiate with myself."

Whoa. It sounds like the state department and a bunch of terrorists. I've negotiated with myself so many times in the past twenty-four hours I need an app to track it.

But the truth is that when we do not negotiate with ourselves, and we fully decide to do something, when we kill all the other options, when we know our *why* and we're fueled with the truth and energy in our heart, **we can do anything**.

We will connect minds. We will open hearts. *And when you point that magic towards helping the world in some way, the impact goes supernova.*

Tramps Like Us

Over these pages I've riffed and rambled about all kinds of things. We've talked about emotional perspective and cognitive dissonance. We've explored the concept of kintsugi and golden repair. We've spun up the magical aspects of storytelling + a bunch of other big ideas.

But I forgot to tell you one very important thing. This is not likely to happen. But it absolutely could.

When you finish this book, literally everything that you learned could disappear from your brain. Just vanish forever into the ethers.

But here's the thing. You can keep one idea with you for the rest of your life. So please take a

minute and write down at least
one big idea/ one major takeaway
that you wanna save in your
brain and heart and bones.
Forever.

…

Okay, good job! I'm sure you got
a great one.

So here's the scoop…

You may be the queen or king of
pain.

You may be sharing a drink
called loneliness.

They may have tried to get you
to go to rehab but you said 'Oh,
hell no."

But you gotta express yourself.

Sweet dreams are made of this stuff.

We need some R-E-S-P-E-C-T.

And even if you're taking the midnight train going anywhere, keep believin'.

It's a long trip. And a strange trip. And a magical mystery tour.

But you never know, you just might find that you get what you need.

Together, Wendie, we can live through this madness.

Because tramps like us, baby, we were born to write.

Some might call me a dreamer, but I know I'm not the only one.

Are you with me?

F yeah!!!

Thanks for reading! Want more magic?

Time to blast some inspiration into your conference, company or organization? I've been known to open the hearts and connect the minds of authors, screenwriters, songwriters, marketers and advertisers (and many others).

I riff and rock the thoughts in this book as a keynote. It's fun. I even do a magic trick.

Or click into the magic to learn more about 1:1 and group coaching. And/ or my workshops.

JeffLeisawitz.com

Thanks for reading. I really appreciate it. And your magic.

I look forward to connecting minds and opening hearts with you soon…

~Jeff

Extra Thanks!

This book started as a little tickle in my brain, but it took the genius of many to bring this thing to the world.

Megan Hills for the amazing, superfun illustrations. Mom for spotting *nearly* every freaking typo.

And to all of the brilliant and beautiful humans who helped me tweak the magic with your amazing brains and shining hearts.

Aaron English
Amy Climber
Beth Inglish
Family!
Jen Hersman
Ken Gunn
Matthew Woodget
Matt Poepsel
Richard Walter
Scott Andrew James
Stacy Bookman
Steve Butcher
Susanna Katzman
Shayla Malek
Tim Hepp
Tim Jones
Wendie Hipolito

And especially, thank *you* for reading!

Jeff Leisawitz is a Cannes Lion, Grand LIA and Clio Gold award winning Creative Consultant, an in-demand keynote speaker, critically acclaimed author, internationally distributed screenwriter and life coach for StoryTellers and Creatives of every flavor. Authors. Screenwriters. Songwriters. Marketers. Advertiser. (And everyone else with a story to tell.)

Jeff is also an award-winning musician/ producer, a former college songwriting instructor, and founding music journalist at KNDD, 107.7 FM, the radio station that broke grunge music to the world.

Jeff burns with a mission—to inspire, teach and coach the magical aspects of storytelling.

Want more words? Read Jeff's first critically acclaimed book *Not F*ing Around—The No Bullsh*t Guide for Getting Your Creative Dreams Off the Ground.*

Printed in Great Britain
by Amazon

32309014R00062